Apple

P9-CEU-501

WATERFORD TOWNSHIP
PUBLIC LIBRARY

A CAREER AS A
CARPENTER

Greg Roza

ROSEN
PUBLISHING®

NEW YORK

Published in 2011 by The Rosen Publishing Group, Inc.
29 East 21st Street, New York, NY 10010

Library of Congress Cataloging-in-Publication Data

Roza, Greg.
A career as a carpenter / Greg Roza.—1st ed.
    p. cm.—(Essential careers)
Includes bibliographical references and index.
ISBN 978-1-4358-9472-3 (library binding)
1. Carpentry—Vocational guidance—Juvenile literature. I. Title.
TH5608.8.R69 2011
694.023—dc22

                                                      2009039998

Manufactured in the United States of America

CPSIA Compliance Information: Batch #S10YA: For Further Information Contact Rosen Publishing, New York, New York
at 1-800-237-9932

contents

INTRO

Carpenters handle all kinds of tasks in the construction of a house, from building walls and roofs, to crafting delicate touches like the decorative mantle shown here.

DUCTION

For thousands of years, carpenters have built and rebuilt our world. Carpentry skills have been passed from one generation to the next, up to the present day. Over time, the carpentry profession has grown and changed to meet contemporary needs.

For many people, carpentry is a smart and rewarding career choice. Our society will always need carpenters to make homes and buildings. Nearly every step of the homemaking process requires the guidance of skilled carpenters—from pouring a concrete foundation to installing door locks in a finished house. Trained carpenters can almost always find work if they look hard enough. Some get work by placing an advertisement in the local paper or by simply having satisfied customers pass along their name and contact information to others.

Some professions may experience a loss of work during difficult economic times when customers simply don't have the money to buy these goods and services. Even in a poor economy, however, carpenters are needed to construct, repair, and remodel homes, offices, and other buildings. A trained carpenter can flourish in good economic times as well as bad. In addition, a carpenter can also save money by doing his or her own home repairs, rather than hiring someone else. Read on to learn more about carpentry and carpentry professions.

chapter 1

WHAT IS CARPENTRY?

It is difficult to imagine a world without carpenters. They build private homes, public buildings, and sometimes help construct new roads and bridges. They build furniture for us to sit on, shelves to store our books, and cabinets to hold our kitchenware. Carpenters also build things that other people need to do their jobs—they may repair a barn for a farmer, build a desk for a writer, or work on constructing an office building. Some carpenters have full-time jobs, while others do freelance work. Some carpenters act as their own boss and have their own shops or businesses.

Traditionally, carpenters only worked with wood. Today's carpenters, however, also work with many other types of materials. Modern building projects often require carpenters to work with supplies such as vinyl siding, electrical wiring, plumbing fixtures, bricks and stones, and roofing tiles. Not every carpenter is proficient with these materials—some prefer to stick with wood projects. However, it is easier for carpenters that can work with a wide range of building materials to land a job.

As with any other career path, there are basic techniques and skills all carpenters should know. However, the specific skills a carpenter needs to master depends on the job he or she needs to tackle. For example, a carpenter might specialize in cabinetmaking and building furniture. The skills required for cabinetmaking are different from the skills needed to build the frame of a house. So, while one carpenter may use hand tools to craft cabinets, chairs, and tables, another may prefer to use power tools to build the frames of new homes. Many skilled carpenters do both!

Carpenters are good at working with their hands, and they receive a great deal of satisfaction from building and repairing things. They like to work with machines and are often capable of fixing them when they break down. Most carpenters prefer to work in the field, rather than at a desk in an office. Today, carpentry is the most popular career choice in the American construction industry. According to the U.S. Bureau of Labor Statistics, there were nearly 1.5 million carpentry positions in 2006. This number is expected to rise in the coming years. If you think a career in carpentry is a good choice, you will have numerous jobs to choose from once you have gained the proper training.

CARPENTRY THROUGH THE AGES

People have relied on carpentry skills for centuries. The word "carpenter" comes from the ancient Romans. Skilled

This is part of an ancient Roman funeral stele, *or gravestone, for a carpenter. It shows two men sawing wood.*

TOOLS OF THE TRADE

Carpenters are trained to use a variety of tools for the sanding, shaping, cutting, and assembly of wooden products. By far the most important carpentry tool is the hammer. Most carpenters carry one with them at all times. Likewise, a carpenter's tool belt often includes basic tools like screwdrivers, wrenches, and a tape measure. These are the tools a carpenter may need at any moment during a typical job.

Power tools can make a carpenter's job easier. Depending on the job, many carpenters choose to carry a nail gun instead of a hammer. Roofers in particular prefer to use nail guns. Carpenters use power drills to drill holes and put in screws. Power saws, too, are vital to modern carpentry. Some, like the circular saw, are portable and easy to handle; others, such as the table saw, are stationary but very versatile.

All carpenters need to have a thorough understanding of the tools of the trade to excel at their profession. Carpenters are often mechanically inclined, which means that they have a talent for working with machines. Many carpenters are capable of maintaining and repairing their own machines and tools.

woodworkers, known as *carpentarius* (Latin for "chariot makers"), traveled with the Roman army. They built and repaired chariots, wagons, and other wooden supplies. They also built forts, outposts, and shelters for the soldiers. Sometimes they even built bridges that the army used to cross rivers.

Many of the tools and techniques used by modern carpenters are based on those invented centuries ago, in the Middle Ages. The tools used by carpenters back then—such as axes,

This carpenter is using a circular saw to construct stairs on a job site. The circular saw is a highly mobile and valuable power tool. Most need to be plugged into an electrical socket, but some come with their own battery.

hammers, and saws—are the same tools that modern-day carpenters use. Some medieval carpenters, commonly called joiners, developed carpentry methods that did not require nails. These methods are still used today, although joiners are now commonly called finish carpenters.

Although today's carpentry is often much the same as the carpentry practiced hundreds of years ago, advances in technology and carpentry techniques have allowed carpenters to perform their jobs more efficiently. Carpenters today still use hammers and handsaws, but they also use circular saws, nail guns, and table saws to make their jobs easier and to do more precise work. Building materials have also changed. Carpenters still work with wood, but they work with modern building materials such as fiberglass, plastic, and drywall.

Many different kinds of carpenters may work together on a modern construction site alongside dozens of other professionals, such as crane operators, electricians, foremen, plumbers, and welders. Some carpenters specialize in a specific type of work, and others tackle a wide range of carpentry projects every day. No matter what the job is, today's carpenters have their work cut out for them!

Basic Skills

Carpenters must be good with tools and must understand modern building techniques. They must also be able to adapt to any situation with the tools and skills available to them. These are the skills and techniques that people learn while training to become a carpenter. Some skills, however, are more basic and are sometimes overlooked. These skills and personality traits can greatly help carpenters excel at their craft.

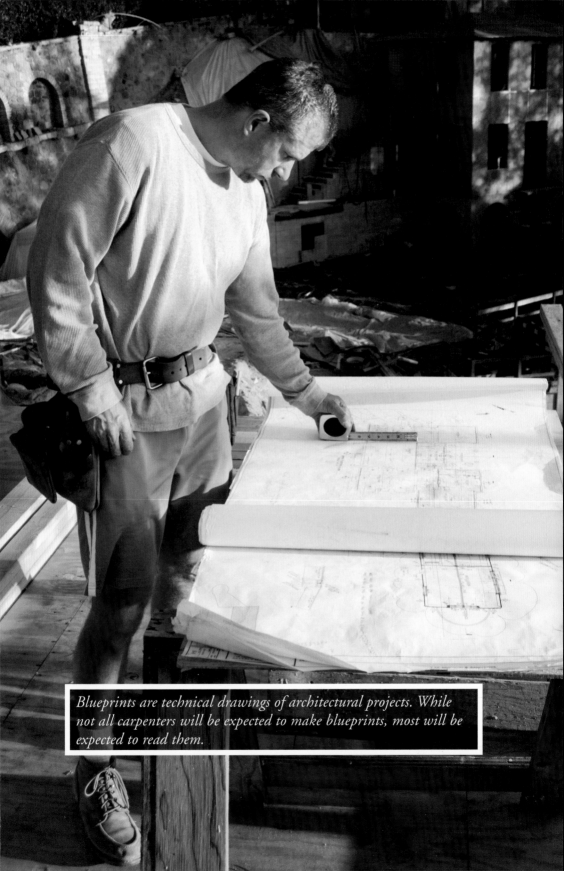

Blueprints are technical drawings of architectural projects. While not all carpenters will be expected to make blueprints, most will be expected to read them.

PHYSICAL FITNESS

Carpentry is definitely a "hands-on" profession. It helps to be physically fit in a career where much of the working day may

The carpenter in this photo is using a tape measure and a speed square to mark a piece of lumber. The tape measure gives the length in feet and inches. The speed square allows the carpenter to draw a straight, even line.

be spent lifting lumber or swinging a hammer. Physical fitness can also help reduce the chances of accidents and injuries, especially in dangerous environments. People who are considering a career as a carpenter may want to join a gym or play a sport in their free time. Working on a busy job site will also help a carpenter stay in shape.

BEING A GOOD COMMUNICATOR

Being able to communicate clearly with others is an important trait for carpenters. On a job site, carpenters are in frequent contact with many other types of workers. They need to be able to listen attentively to instructions, give clear directions, and answer questions. They also often have to read and create building designs called blueprints. Some may be required to write reports or business letters, or they might be in frequent contact with the customer who hired them for the job.

MATH

Carpenters frequently use math skills in the course of their workday. Math skills are needed for making measurements, estimating the materials needed to finish a job, and much more. Carpenters must often add and subtract fractions and decimals. They must also have a good grasp of geometric applications. It is good to be a quick carpenter, but precision and care while measuring is far more important. This is reflected in the carpenter's adage: Measure twice, cut once. In many cases, if a carpenter's measurements are off by just one-sixteenth of an inch, the quality of the project will suffer.

SAFETY

Although carpentry is one of the most popular jobs in the United States, it is also one of the most dangerous. To reduce the chance of job-site accidents, carpenters need to pay attention to their surroundings, wear protective clothing, and respect their equipment.

Carpentry tools—especially power tools—can be very dangerous when safety guidelines are ignored. Likewise, carpenters sometimes work in dangerous environments, where they must adhere to safety standards to ensure that they don't get injured. Carpenters learn to watch out for others on the job site while working, and to be mindful of construction vehicles and heavy machinery. They wear protective gear and always make sure to learn the proper way to use and maintain tools and machines before attempting to operate them.

Hard hats, thick gloves, goggles, and ear protectors are examples of essential safety gear worn by carpenters.

chapter 2

CARPENTRY EDUCATION

It's never too early to begin learning how to be a carpenter. Some people manage to learn enough to become a carpenter without earning a high school diploma. However, workers without a high school diploma are often at a disadvantage when competing for carpentry jobs. Beyond simply getting a high school education, many people decide to seek formal carpentry training.

There are numerous learning opportunities that prospective carpenters can pursue before graduating from high school. Working in a hardware store or home remodeling store is a great way to become familiar with the tools and supplies of the construction trades. Some students also volunteer to help build and repair homes and parks in their communities. Activities such as these help supplement formal training and look great on a résumé.

HIGH SCHOOL CLASSES

Doing well in high school is the first step toward attaining a career in carpentry. Subjects such as math, English, physical education, and art will help prepare students for just about any career, and carpentry is no exception. Earning a high school diploma will also make your résumé more attractive to potential employers.

This sixth grader in New Haven, Connecticut, is making a birdhouse in her technical education class. Notice that she is wearing goggles to protect her eyes.

For many people, a career in carpentry begins with technical education, or tech ed, classes. Modern tech ed classes have come a long way since the days when high school students learned the basics of how to use tools in what was simply called "shop class." Today, students receive a more comprehensive view of technological instruction. Topics covered in a tech ed class often not only include carpentry and woodworking, but also computer drawing, building construction, and mechanics.

Of course, many high schools still offer general industrial arts classes. These classes focus on single topics often included in technological education, and may include woodworking, metalworking, and building construction. The more industrial arts classes a student takes, the better prepared he or she will be to work in the field.

Most carpenters are expected to know how to read blueprints, diagrams, and plans, so it is important to take mechanical drawing and drafting courses. High school mechanical drawing courses introduce students to the basics of reading and creating blueprints. Many of these courses also include technical drawing instruction, which can help aspiring carpenters get ahead in today's construction industry.

CAREER SCHOOLS

Some teens are fortunate enough to attend schools that offer career-related classes in addition to standard coursework. These are sometimes called career schools or career academies. Most career schools specialize in a particular career area, such as accounting, agriculture, health, or law. A number of career schools across the country also offer carpentry and other construction-related coursework. Career schools can prepare young people for a job, or for the higher education needed for a particular career.

Construction career schools are often supported by businesses and organizations in the construction industry. They receive funding and supplies from businesses to help them train students. Students are required to complete standard high

This student builds a roof at Dunedin High School's Academy of Architectural Design and Building Technologies in Dunedin, Florida. Programs like this one are designed to prepare students for a long-term vocation.

school courses, but those courses are often taught in the context of the construction industry. In addition, smaller groups of students work together over a period of two years in their chosen craft. During this time, they benefit from guest speakers, hands-on training, and field trips.

HIGHER EDUCATION

Beyond high school, there are several ways to pursue an education in carpentry. Some people go on to become successful carpenters without any kind of formal education at all, but it is rare. In today's world, a degree or certificate of training is much more attractive to potential employers than experience alone.

VOCATIONAL SCHOOLS

Vocational schools (also called trade schools) teach a wide range of career skills, including carpentry. Some people attend vocational school during their last few years of high school. Others attend after graduating. The main purpose of a trade school is to train students for a career, or vocation. Trade schools can be an invaluable resource for young men and women who want to secure a future in the world of carpentry.

GREG MOSKAL: TECHNICAL EDUCATION TEACHER

Greg Moskal has been a teacher in Central Square, New York, for more than ten years. He has a master's degree in technical education. In addition, he has had a lifetime of experience in building construction, carpentry, and art.

How did you first get involved with carpentry?
Carpentry was a big part of my life growing up. My family built our home, a log cabin, when I was ten. After high school, I got a summer carpentry job with a small outfit. I learned a great deal through one-on-one instruction. I had the opportunity to do many different types of jobs—from small home repairs to building entire houses from start to finish.

Besides teaching, how do you make use of your carpentry skills?
I use my carpentry skills to generate a supplemental income. There is always an opportunity for work. Through networking, I have had the opportunity to help build the homes of some traditional artisans. These people are extremely skilled in traditional joinery where the building frame is held together without a single nail. I have worked with other trained carpenters on timber frame barn restorations and furniture. I repair my own home, which would otherwise be very costly. I also find great enjoyment [in] making furniture and crafts.

What advice would you give to youths interested in pursuing a career in carpentry?
Start with basic technology classes. Technical drawing is a must for people who want to become carpenters. Most high schools

have basic woodworking, carpentry, and residential structure classes. For more in-depth knowledge, students can look into local vocational schools. Students can also look for summer work with a local contractor. Small-time contractors usually give the broadest exposure to different aspects of carpentry and building. Larger firms offer more specialized carpentry. Students may also have a family member or friend who would be willing to mentor them.

Students don't need a carpentry background to enroll in a trade school, but they do need to select the type of training that they want to pursue. For example, a student may decide to pursue a residential or commercial carpentry degree. Residential carpentry courses focus on the skills required to build homes, such as drywall installation and roofing. In commercial carpentry courses, students might learn how to install suspended ceilings and office cubicles.

It should be mentioned that, outside of school, probably the best way to secure a carpentry career is to become an apprentice. Hands-on work with a trained expert is the most efficient way to sharpen your skills and learn about the profession. Many vocational schools and colleges offer apprenticeship programs, as do carpentry unions.

COLLEGES

Colleges across the United States offer carpentry degrees. The required coursework for these degrees is often very similar to what one would receive in a trade school. In fact, some trade schools have begun to offer college degrees in addition to job training.

To earn a college degree, students are usually expected to take courses in a number of different subjects, such as English composition, math, and psychology. Many of these courses can be very useful to someone who desires a career in carpentry.

A carpentry instructor at Iowa Central Community College discusses a project with his students. He is showing the students drawings of the building they are about to begin constructing.

Colleges may also offer courses on modern, cutting-edge topics that might not be part of a trade school's curriculum, such as classes about environmental issues or green building design. Although college can be a financial burden for many people, there are scholarships and grants available for people who need them. Some scholarships are specifically intended for carpentry students.

INTERNSHIPS

Before earning a degree in carpentry, students might be expected to complete an internship. Internships help students make the transition from college life to the working world. Although interns are usually not paid for their work, they benefit by working with experienced professionals in successful businesses. This is one of the best ways for a college student with little professional experience to learn carpentry skills. Internships are generally shorter and more informal than apprenticeships, and some internships can count for college credit. Another great benefit to internships is that the companies that offer internships sometimes hire the people they've trained after graduation.

OTHER OPTIONS

Some people don't end up going to college. Instead, they travel, do volunteer work, or find a permanent job. Getting a college

This Job Corps building and maintenance instructor is teaching a student how to repair and refinish old furniture.

education is always a big help when it comes to advancing one's career, but it is not the only option. Luckily, high school graduates who choose not to attend college have many choices when it comes to their future.

THE MILITARY

Many young people choose to enter the military or the military reserves after graduation. Just as in the civilian world, carpenters are needed in the military. After basic military training, recruits interested in carpentry receive specialized training. Upon being discharged from the military, veterans can apply the training they received to their carpentry career.

JOB CORPS

The Job Corps is a vocational training program for young people ages sixteen to twenty-four. It is managed by the U.S. Department of Labor. This program gives youths from low-income families a chance to be trained in a wide range of vocations, including carpentry. The Job Corps also offers tutoring programs for students that want to earn their diploma or GED, provides mentoring programs, and helps its participants

In 2005, Hurricane Katrina destroyed many homes in New Orleans, Louisiana. Volunteers, shown here, help rebuild homes as part of a Habitat for Humanity project.

create solid résumés. Although not everyone can attend the Job Corps, it provides many with valuable vocational training. The program is free for those who qualify.

VOLUNTEERING

Some volunteer programs also offer people the opportunity to learn carpentry. By volunteering for a nonprofit organization like Habitat for Humanity, which builds and restores homes for families in need of shelter around the world, young people can learn valuable carpentry skills while assessing if this career is right for them. The Peace Corps also offers people the opportunity to volunteer their carpentry skills for a good cause. However, the organization expects applicants to already have some experience in the field. Along with proper carpentry training and certification, the experience that a person gains while volunteering can help him or her climb the career ladder.

CORRESPONDENCE AND ONLINE COURSES

Finally, some people seek training from correspondence courses and online courses. This can be a good way to learn about carpentry, but it also has certain drawbacks. For instance, not all correspondence courses offer national certification. Certified carpenters have received up-to-date instruction from an officially recognized training organization, and they have the certificate to prove it. Some training programs offer national certification, while others offer certification based on a particular state or region.

People who learn online also won't receive hands-on training, which is the best way to learn when it comes to carpentry. Anyone who is thinking of signing up for an online or correspondence course should be sure he or she understands exactly what the course offers.

FIND A MENTOR

A mentor is someone who has accumulated the knowledge necessary to become an expert in something. Mentors pass their knowledge and experience on to others who hope to become proficient in the same area. They are often, but not always, older than the people they train. Some people are lucky enough to know someone who is willing to mentor them as they learn carpentry skills. A mentor such as a parent, relative, or family friend can help an aspiring carpenter become familiar with the tools and proper techniques of carpentry. Regardless of the career path they hope to follow, young and inexperienced carpenters can gain knowledge and expertise through the guidance of a skilled veteran.

chapter 3

APPRENTICESHIPS AND CERTIFICATION

As carpentry students gain experience, they find that they can accomplish many tasks with confidence. The more work that they do, the better they will become at their job. When it comes to establishing a long-term career in carpentry, however, personal experience may not be enough. Many (if not most) employers expect carpenters to be certified.

Many carpenters simply become certified in general carpentry. Others choose to become certified in a more specific type of carpentry, such as rough framing or pile driving. Still others become certified in several different areas. Certification makes carpenters more valuable to employers and makes it easier for them to find work. An apprenticeship is one of the best ways to earn a carpentry certification.

APPRENTICESHIPS

Carpenters learned their craft through apprenticeship for centuries, long before universities taught carpentry courses. Apprenticeship is a method of training that generally combines hands-on, work-site experience with classroom instruction. Many professionals will say the best way to

This journeyman is an experienced finish carpenter. He is using a miter saw on a job site to make precise cuts. Journeypersons like this one can teach apprentices everything they need to know to become a professional carpenter.

become a carpenter is to apprentice with an experienced journeyman or journeyperson.

Journeypersons have completed an apprenticeship program and have become certified carpenters. They pass on the skills, techniques, and knowledge they have accumulated during their career to their apprentices. A journeyperson makes sure that his or her apprentice spends time on many different tasks on the work site. In this way, the apprentice gains valuable experience and a well-rounded education.

Another great benefit of apprenticeships is that apprentices earn a salary while being trained. Most college internships do not pay a salary, which can make it difficult for young people trying to start a career. Many students with internships need to get an additional job or two to pay their living expenses. With an apprenticeship, however, students are often paid for their work. The beginning pay is usually only about half of what a journeyperson makes, but the pay goes up as the apprentice gains knowledge and experience. In some cases, apprentices may also receive health benefits.

WHAT TO EXPECT

Most apprenticeship programs last for four years, or about the same time it would take to receive a bachelor's degree in college. However, it is possible for some apprentices to finish a program in less time.

Carpentry apprenticeships cover a wide range of specialties, such as rough carpentry, cabinetmaking, shipbuilding, acoustical tile installation, and stage and prop creation. Unlike apprenticeships of the past, modern apprenticeships often include classroom instruction. Required class work may include courses in mathematics, geometry, and mechanics, among other basic courses.

WHAT IS PREAPPRENTICESHIP?

In most states, you must be seventeen before you can become an apprentice. In some states, you must be eighteen. Preapprenticeship programs are often much like classes offered in vocational schools;

An experienced journeyman (right) *gives his apprentice guidance on the job site.*

in fact, many trade schools offer this type of program, as do some high schools. A preapprenticeship simply prepares someone for an apprenticeship and increases the chances of being accepted before other people who are the same age but have less experience because they have not been through

such a program. The Job Corps, mentioned in the previous chapter, is sometimes considered a pre-apprenticeship program. For more information about pre-apprenticeship programs, contact your local carpenters union.

It's possible to make it without being an apprentice first, but it may not be easy. Being a competent worker with solid experience helps, but it is not always enough. Most organizations that employ teams of carpenters—particularly commercial and residential construction firms—will require the certification that results from an apprenticeship program.

Uncertified carpenters might be lucky enough to land a job with a small local business, especially if they know someone who can help them out. Some carpenters start their own private businesses and do very well. However, it still usually takes years of fieldwork to gain the expertise required to run a private carpentry business.

COMPLETING AN APPRENTICESHIP

Some carpentry training programs involve getting a two-year associate's degree, which is then followed by a two-year apprenticeship. For others, class work and fieldwork are carried out in stages. An apprentice is expected to show aptitude at one skill stage before he or she can move on to the next. The table below shows the hours needed for each stage of three different carpentry-related apprenticeships provided by the United Brotherhood of Carpenters union.

General Carpentry

General Knowledge	350 to 500 hours
Concrete Framework	975 to 1,500 hours
Wood Framing	975 to 1,500 hours
Metal Framing	650 to 1,000 hours
Exterior Finish	650 to 1,000 hours
Interior Finish	650 to 1,000 hours
Supplemental Skills	975 to 1,500 hours
Total	**5,200 to 8,000 hours**

Cabinetmaker

General Knowledge	350 to 500 hours
Machining	1,430 to 2,200 hours
Assembly	1,625 to 2,500 hours
Surface Preparation and Finish	650 to 1,000 hours
Installation	975 to 1,500 hours
Supplemental Skills	195 to 300 hours
Total	**5,200 to 8,000 hours**

Pile Driver	
General Knowledge	325 to 500 hours
Concrete Framework	1,300 to 2,000 hours
Pile Installation	975 to 1,500 hours
Foundation, Shoring, and Underpinning Systems	975 to 1,500 hours
Metal	975 to 1,500 hours
Supplemental Skills	650 to 1,000 hours
Total	**5,200 to 8,000 hours**

CARPENTRY UNIONS

Most apprenticeships are offered by carpentry unions— in fact, when someone begins an apprenticeship, he or she will probably be expected to join the local union. All regional carpentry unions are members of the United Brotherhood of Carpenters (UBC).

A union is an organization of workers within a specific profession. There are unions for carpenters, electricians, clothing manufacturers, bakers, musicians, teachers, actors, writers, and many other professions. Unions are

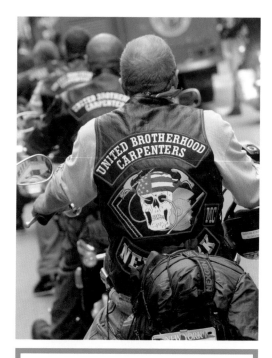

Members of the UBC ride motorcycles in Manhattan during the 2009 Labor Day Parade.

Not only was Peter J. McGuire the founder of the UBC, he was also one of the leading figures of the labor movement of the late 1800s. In 1882, he proposed the idea of making Labor Day a national holiday.

important and powerful organizations designed to uphold the rights of workers. Prior to the existence of unions in the United States, workers had little or no rights in the workplace. Most workers—skilled and unskilled—were paid very little, worked under very dangerous conditions, had no benefits, and had no say in how business was conducted. The establishment of unions gave workers a voice in the workplace.

Union members are expected to pay dues to fund union activities. However, the benefits of joining a union are often well worth the cost. In addition to bargaining for excellent health benefits, fair working hours, and pay raises, carpentry unions offer the best training available. It takes eight thousand hours, or about four years, to finish the union apprenticeship program. Completion of the program results in national accreditation.

THE UNITED BROTHERHOOD OF CARPENTERS AND JOINERS OF AMERICA

The United Brotherhood of Carpenters and Joiners of America—commonly called the United Brotherhood of Carpenters, or UBC—is the largest building trades union in North America. It was founded in 1881 by a journeyperson named Peter J. McGuire who wanted to give a voice to carpenters all over the country. The late nineteenth century was a time of great industrial growth in the United States. Like most workers at the time, carpenters usually worked long hours in dangerous conditions for little pay.

(continued on page 38)

After several successful strikes in the mid- to late 1880s, the UBC grew larger and more powerful. Although the union would face frequent struggles in the decades to come, it helped establish work standards for trained carpenters in the United States. Thanks to the UBC, carpentry has become a highly viable and desirable career option for young workers.

Today, the UBC has more than half a million members. Member training is one of the UBC's greatest concerns, along with continuing to ensure that carpenters are treated fairly in the workplace. New techniques, tools, and regulations have placed new demands on carpenters in the United States. UBC journeyperson apprentice training programs have allowed union carpenters to keep up with modern technology.

CERTIFICATION

Once an apprentice completes an apprenticeship program sponsored by the UBC, he or she becomes certified for carpentry work. This means that the apprentice receives a nationally recognized certificate and is allowed to work anywhere in the United States. Some apprenticeship programs may grant carpenters certification in one state only. Make sure you know what type of certification you will earn upon finishing an apprenticeship. It is always best to choose one with national accreditation if possible.

If carpentry students want to expand their horizons, they can seek additional training in another area and earn a new certificate. For example, job sites often need people to build scaffolding, which requires workers with scaffolding certificates. Becoming certified in additional areas means engaging in another training program. This can take time and money, but it is usually worth it. A carpenter certified in many different areas will be able to work many different types of jobs.

chapter 4

STARTING A CAREER IN CARPENTRY

Once a carpenter has been trained and certified, the next step is to find a job. This can seem like an overwhelming process for someone who's never had a job, but it doesn't have to be. Finding a job is sometimes as easy as walking into a business and asking if they are hiring. Job seekers who are confident, persistent, and professional are often successful when it comes to getting work.

People with a carpentry diploma or certificate are more likely to be interviewed by carpentry and construction operations. Organizations and schools that train carpenters often help them find employment after graduating. Many apprenticeships and internships result in full-time work with the organization participating in the program. It is a wise decision to take advantage of job placement offers after training is completed.

STARTING OUT

Before looking for a job, it is a good idea to get a notebook and jot down short-term and long-term goals. A short-term goal might be to get a job at a hardware store within a year. Long-term goals are often less specific. For young people, this is usually because they aren't exactly sure what they want to be doing in five to ten years. Someone might write, "I want to be a carpenter." That's a great long-term goal. Another person might have a specific goal, such as, "I want to be a rough carpenter working for a residential construction company." Young people often end up revising their initial long-term goals, and

Many cities have career centers, like this one in Oakland, California. Career centers offer instruction in interview techniques, résumé writing, and many other career areas. The people here are checking a board with current employment openings.

that's perfectly normal. As people get older and gain more experience, their long-term goals become more concrete.

Start looking for a job by checking the classified section of the local newspaper. Job listings online are also helpful. Other job resources include the local employment office and career fairs. As previously mentioned, many people inquire about positions in places they would hope to work. This often involves filling out a job application, so it's important to always come prepared. Most businesses ask for basic personal information, as well as social and professional references (people they can call to find out more about the applicant) and a job history. Job applicants may be asked to provide the names and contact information of their former employers.

WHAT IS NETWORKING?

Another great way to find a job is to rely on a network. Have you ever heard the phrase "You scratch my back and I'll scratch yours"? This saying means that if you do me a favor, I'll do a favor for you. This is the main idea behind social and professional networks.

Networking is the process of creating business opportunities by

It's important to stay in touch with the people in your network, even if there's presently nothing you need from them. It's also a good idea to offer to do favors for the people in your network from time to time.

collecting and organizing social and business contacts. The purpose of this network is to form a collection of people that can be called upon when the need arises.

The longer someone works on building a career, the larger his or her network will grow. A well-maintained network can help a person attain his or her professional goals, whether that's getting a raise, getting a loan to start a business, or just getting a good deal on building supplies. A carpenter's network may include other carpenters, contractors, hardware store owners, lumber suppliers, or tool manufacturers.

Writing a Résumé

A résumé is an essential tool for anyone hoping to establish a career after graduating from high school. Since it is the first glimpse an employer will get of a potential worker, a résumé needs to be neat, precise, and informative.

In a nutshell, a good résumé should include relevant educational and professional experiences listed in chronological order on a single sheet of paper. The information on a résumé is generally concise and to the point, and includes the applicant's personal strengths and talents, especially those that an employer would consider to be assets. Some people refer to résumé-writing guides that are available online and at the library when creating their résumé. Others choose to have a professional writer prepare their résumé or enlist the help of a friend or family member with résumé-writing experience.

Besides listing the applicant's education and relevant job experience, a résumé should list any specialized training, apprenticeships, internships, or other experience pertaining to the job the applicant is trying to get. A carpenter might have different résumés depending on the type of carpentry job. For instance, a résumé that is put together with a commercial or residential building job in mind might be different from a

Take the time to craft a solid résumé. Employers are likely to pass over résumés that are poorly written, sloppy, or have misspelled words. Many professionals rewrite their résumés frequently, even when they aren't looking for a job.

résumé aimed at getting a job such as house remodeling, building scaffolding, or another specialty job.

Employers generally expect to receive a cover letter with a résumé. Just as with a résumé, a cover letter should contain very specific information. Writers should begin their cover letter by introducing themselves and stating why they are sending a résumé. The body of the cover letter should highlight educational and professional experience that would make them a good fit for the job. It may be OK to e-mail a résumé and cover letter, but always make sure before sending it. Some employers prefer job applicants to fax or mail their résumé and cover letter.

INTERVIEWS

After getting an employer's attention with a well-written résumé and cover letter, an applicant may be asked to come in for an interview. Not all interviews follow the same format or deal with the same issues. One interview might take place in an office, whereas another might take place on a construction site. No matter where the interview takes place, it is a good idea to follow basic rules of etiquette. Being courteous and polite will greatly improve a job applicant's chance of landing a job.

Before going on an interview, a job applicant should research the company so he or she can answer any questions related to its business. An applicant should know the name of his or her interviewer and use it in the interview and should always treat the interviewer with respect. Interviewers want to hear job applicants talk about themselves and reveal their knowledge and expertise. Applicants should maintain eye contact and speak clearly.

First impressions count for everything when applying for a job. It's important that job applicants dress well for interviews. It is not always necessary to wear a suit, but neat and clean clothes are a must. It's also important to shake hands with the interviewer before and after the interview.

WOMEN IN CARPENTRY

The majority of carpenters are men. However, this does not mean that women who want to become carpenters should feel discouraged in any way. The same career options available to men are also available to women. In some respects, women may face more difficulties than men while pursuing a carpentry career. Some women may find it intimidating to work in a male-dominated industry. However, there are many success stories to inspire young women who choose that career path.

In 1935, Margaret Ellings became the first woman to join the United Brotherhood of Carpenters. Since then, the number of female carpenters has grown steadily. In 2009, there were about twenty thousand female carpenters in the UBC. Today, many female carpenters are members of Sisters in the Brotherhood, which is part of the UBC. The Sisters in the Brotherhood hold frequent conferences to help recruit new female carpenters.

Some colleges may offer carpentry courses specifically for women, but by and large the training process for women is no different than the one for men. In addition, thanks to groups like the Sisters in the Brotherhood, there has been a push to hire more women in the trade industries.

Interviewers will often conclude the interview by saying that they will "be in touch," but an applicant should still ask when they might hear from them. This helps show that the applicant is interested in beginning work. Also, it is usually good etiquette to send a follow-up letter several days after the interview. Follow-up letters should generally be short and not too formal. Job seekers shouldn't wait around for an answer from one business before going on their next interview. Going to as many interviews as possible increases a person's chances of landing a job.

This female carpenter is working on a construction site in New York City. She has been a carpenter for more than twenty years.

GETTING THE JOB

Newly hired workers usually go through a period of training where they learn how the business is run. Although a person's first days at a new job can be nerve-wracking, the butterflies soon pass, and the newly hired worker becomes accustomed to the job. In time, workers may earn enough respect from managers, foremen, and supervisors to get raises, promotions, and other benefits. These are necessary steps in establishing a serious carpentry career.

When people choose a career, they hope that the work they do will be in demand for a long time to come. Carpenters have always been in high demand and constitute about half of the laborers in today's construction industry. Finding a job is just the first step down the road of a lifelong career, but it is an important step. After getting a job, a carpenter can begin to prepare for the future.

chapter 5

MAKING A LIVING

Anyone interested in becoming a carpenter can match his or her interests and skills to a rewarding career. A wide range of career paths are available to carpenters, depending on their interest, experience, and skill set. Each of the carpentry careers discussed in this chapter can be pursued in an apprenticeship program.

ROUGH FRAMER

The first carpenters to work on a job site are usually the rough framers, also called rough carpenters or simply framers. Framers create the support structures for buildings, which requires them to work not only with wood, but also with other types of materials. For instance, many modern wall frames are made of metal beams.

The most common framing jobs involve building the frames for walls, floors, and roofs. These frames form the "skeleton" which the rest of the building is constructed around. Framers also build the forms (or molds) used to pour concrete structures, as well as the chutes used to transfer concrete into the forms. Other jobs may include making support structures when building tunnels, replacing rotten wood in old homes, and digging holes for support posts.

Rough framers must be able to read blueprints and diagrams and use them to build frameworks, forms, scaffolds, supports,

This rough framer is constructing a frame that will be used to hold concrete for the fiftieth floor of a building in New York City.

and many other rough structures. They must be quick yet precise when measuring, cutting, and assembling lumber. If the angles and sizes of their frames are not perfect, the materials that are added later will not fit properly. To achieve exact measurements, framers use tape measures, levels, squares, and plumb bobs.

FINISHER

If a rough carpenter is the first person on a job site, the finisher is often the last. As the name suggests, finishers put the final touches on a home. They build, assemble, and install the decorative elements that make a structure look pleasant and ready to be lived in. The most common finishing jobs are cutting and installing wood trim for doors and windows and molding for walls and floors. These are the pieces that cover rough edges and corners. Finishers are sometimes called trim carpenters.

Cutting molding and trim is precise work. Angles and measurements need to be perfect to ensure that the finished product looks appealing. Some finishers specialize in joinery, a method of fitting wood pieces together without using fasteners like nails and screws. Depending on the company and the size of the job, a finisher might also install counters, doors, flooring, railings, stairs, and windows. Many finishers restore older homes, making them look new again.

CABINETMAKER

Cabinetmakers build and repair furniture and cabinets. Sometimes they create objects from scratch; other times they assemble parts that have already been cut and shaped. Cabinetmakers must be good at reading blueprints, diagrams, and instructions. A highly capable cabinetmaker can build a perfect product according to a customer's specifications. Most are very good at repairing broken items as well.

In addition to wood, cabinetmakers work with many other materials, such as Formica, glass, and granite. They must know

The cabinetmaker in this photo is modernizing the kitchen by installing a custom-made kitchen island and cabinets. At the same time, the electrician on the ladder is installing lights inside the cabinets.

how to cut exact joints so that pieces fit together perfectly. They also use sandpaper, glue, wood stains, paint, and shapers to put finishing touches on the items they make. Besides cabinets, they also make items such as racks, shelves, and tables.

FLOOR COVERER

Floor coverers are carpenters that work exclusively with flooring materials. They start their work after plywood subfloors have been installed over the floor frame. Floor coverers must be good at taking accurate measurements and estimating supplies and costs. They work with a variety of materials, including carpet, ceramic tiles, vinyl, and wood. They also have an extensive knowledge of the adhesives, fasteners, and wood stains needed to finish flooring a room. Many floorers are adept at restoring old, worn-out flooring.

INTERIOR SYSTEMS SPECIALIST

Interior systems specialists are most often employed by commercial building contractors. They assemble and install metal frames for ceiling

Millwrights receive training in new technologies that are relevant to their jobs. This millwright is learning how to use a laser alignment instrument at the Arkansas Regional Council of Carpenters training facility in Russellville, Arkansas.

tiles and lights. They also install acoustical tiles, office furnishings, wall partitions, and other items used in commercial buildings. Although most of the time they install prefabricated materials, interior systems specialists should have fabrication and welding skills to help solve unforeseen problems.

MILLWRIGHT

Millwrights install, maintain, and repair machinery. The machines they work with can include conveyor systems, electric sensors, generators, pumps, and turbines. Some millwrights specialize in one specific type of machine. Millwrights need to have a solid understanding of industrial tools and mechanics.

Millwrights set up the necessary machinery for a carpentry job before it begins. While the job is in progress, they maintain the machinery to ensure that work is not interrupted. They oil moving parts, repair machinery when necessary, maintain electrical connections, and refill fuel tanks. They may also be called upon to fabricate new parts on the job site. In addition to the machines themselves, millwrights oversee construction of the foundations needed to support the machinery. They may also be required to instruct workers in the use and care of all machinery on the job site. It's common for a millwright to perform another kind of specialized work, such as serving as a cabinetmaker. When a job is done, millwrights oversee the workers who take apart and move machinery.

PILE DRIVER

A pile driver operates large construction vehicles that pound wood or steel beams into the ground. These beams, called piles, are mainly used to create support systems for large buildings and structures. Along with basic carpentry skills, particularly concrete formwork, pile drivers need to be knowledgeable about topics such as bedrock formations, construction vehicles, foundation materials, metals, and welding.

Besides creating support structures for large buildings, pile drivers also create the foundations for piers and bridges. Pile drivers might be needed to help hold back land during deep excavations. Similarly, they are sometimes used to drive piles that hold back water when creating underwater bridge

These teens are being trained in set design at the Mosaic Youth Theatre in Detroit, Michigan. The Mosaic Youth Theatre is a free program that helps young people develop the skills necessary to pursue a career in stage productions.

and pier foundations. Pile drivers often work alone, but are in frequent contact with engineers, supervisors, and surveyors.

PROP AND STAGE DESIGN

Carpenters interested in working in the entertainment industry might want to help build props and stages. These carpenters are sometimes known as set carpenters. Stage designers and

builders help create sets for amusement parks, movie productions, and theatrical shows. A general carpentry apprenticeship can help people who want to pursue a career in prop and stage design establish themselves. However, there are also prop and stage design apprenticeships.

Some set carpenters will work in a single location, such as a theater or a park. Others, however, will have the opportunity to travel to different locations. This is especially true for carpenters that work on touring theatrical productions or movies. Some movies are filmed entirely on a set, but many are filmed in various locations. Set carpenters often take great pleasure in seeing their creations become an important part of a movie or theatrical production.

Moving Up the Ladder

Trained carpenters have the opportunity to gain promotions or move on to a completely new career. Career changes often come with greater responsibility and more work, but they can also come with more benefits, authority, and a higher salary.

For example, carpenters who have several years of experience working in multiple areas of construction may move up to a supervisory or management position, such as a foreman or project manager. A foreman supervises all workers in his or her trade, so there are always multiple foremen on any large job site. Project managers direct all daily activities onsite, and foremen may report directly to them. Often these positions are available to college graduates with specific training in construction management.

The UBC sponsors a superintendent career training program called the Carpenters International Training Fund's Superintendent Career Training Program (SCTP). This program is similar to the UBC's apprenticeship program. Carpenters are selected for the SCTP based on their experience

BUILDING A HOUSE

From basement to attic, every step of the house-building process requires the guidance and expertise of trained carpenters. Even before construction on a home has begun, carpenters are onsite, building concrete forms out of two-by-fours. Millwrights arrive to set up and maintain the machinery needed for construction. For larger buildings, pile drivers may be needed to dig into the ground and set up support beams for a steady foundation. Some carpenters help make roads and driveways leading to construction sites.

When construction begins, rough framers put up the frame of the house. Carpenters cover the frame with drywall or plaster after the electrical and plumbing systems have been put in place. Flooring specialists lay down subfloors and then cover them with carpet, tile, wood flooring, and other coverings. Cabinetmakers may construct cabinets, furniture, and shelving. Finishers cover the rough edges in walls and floors with molding and trim. Windows and doors are installed, and carpenters lay the house's roof.

Toward the very end of the process, some carpenters install hardware, such as door and cabinet knobs, railings, handles, and door and window locks, as well as adding other finishing touches to the house. Throughout the process, carpenters estimate the cost of building supplies. After a house is built, carpenters might be hired to build external structures such as decks, porches, gazebos, sheds, and garages.

and standing in the union. Participants receive classroom training for eighteen months. After that, they are assigned a mentor who tests them in the field.

BECOMING A CONTRACTOR

Many trained carpenters decide to start their own businesses. Some carpenters choose to run small specialty businesses, such

as a woodshop that specializes in creating and repairing furniture. Other carpenters with extensive commercial and residential building experience choose to become contractors.

A contractor is a person or company that signs a contract to complete a project. Contractors bid on potential carpentry jobs. The contractor that puts in the lowest bid generally gets the job. Contracting is a competitive business, and it can be difficult for small companies and first-time

This foreman is talking to a worker on a job site. It is important for the foreman to keep a close eye on every step of the building process to make sure the job gets completed on time.

contractors to break into the business. Some seasons may be slower than others, so contractors must be prepared to endure occasional financial losses. Still, contractors can make a lot of money if they work hard and build a good reputation for themselves.

There is a lot for carpenters to think about when starting their own business. Businesspeople must understand local laws and regulations. For example, some states require special licenses to do large-scale carpentry and construction; others don't. Business owners in every state must have insurance.

It is in a contractor's best interest to understand all facets of building construction—including carpentry, electrical wiring, plumbing, and so on. Contractors also have to deal with things like billing, hiring employees, and ordering supplies. Some contractors hire foremen and supervisors to help oversee large projects. Starting a business is a lot of work, but for a person who wants to be his or her own boss, it can be worth it.

OTHER CAREER CHOICES

Instead of becoming a contractor, many carpenters choose to become private businesspeople. They place advertisements in the paper and in the Yellow Pages. Most of their time is spent traveling with their tools to homes and buildings to build and repair a wide variety of projects.

Some carpenters choose to become instructors or teachers. Others use their knowledge as purchasing agents working for contractors or even architects. Some specialized carpenters may assemble teams of workers in their area and start their own business. For example, a cabinetmaker may open his or her own shop and bid on construction projects. After getting a job, the team of cabinetmakers that works for the shop would go to job sites and do their job. In short, the career choices for a carpenter are almost limitless.

I Can Fix That

In today's economic climate, not everyone can be guaranteed a steady and secure job. Fortunately, there are usually many different types of jobs that a trained carpenter can apply for, even during tough economic times. Even with a secure full-time job, however, a carpenter can use his or her skills to earn supplemental income by doing smaller jobs on the side. This can especially come in handy when a carpenter needs to catch up on his or her bills, buy new tools and supplies, save up for a vacation, or just wants to make some extra money to buy something special. Depending on a carpenter's experience level, supplementing his or her income can be accomplished in any number of ways—from fixing a neighbor's creaky staircase to building a toolshed for a client.

Most often, carpenters get extra work through word of mouth. Carpenters often hear things like, "I heard you're a carpenter. I've been looking for someone to fix the roof of my garage. How much would you charge for something like that?" Those are exciting words for a carpenter who wants to pick up some extra work. Carpenters can also drum up business by placing an ad in the classified section of the local newspaper or by advertising their services online. Every client that a carpenter does a good job for becomes a valuable connection in his or her network. Any job, no matter how small, might somehow lead to bigger jobs later on. Picking up side work is also a great way to practice the craft of carpentry. Some carpenters choose to start their own business based on the experience they gain doing side jobs.

FUTURE OUTLOOK

The future looks good for carpenters. Despite occasional set-backs in the economy, carpenters are always in high demand.

Carpentry students join their instructor at a construction site. Teachers are responsible for teaching their students modern innovations and green carpentry techniques, in addition to the traditional carpentry skills.

As the demand for new buildings continues, carpenters will be needed at nearly every step of the construction process.

Home remodeling is another lucrative area for carpenters today. Old homes often have problems that can only be

repaired by a trained carpenter. Some carpenters make a good living buying old homes, fixing them up, and selling them for a great profit. The home industry alone sustains literally millions of carpenters.

As technology changes, so does carpentry. New tools, supplies, and techniques have revolutionized the way carpenters do their job. Those who have been in the business for a long time might be required to change and update their craft. New carpenters receive modern training, preparing them for a career in the field.

The push for "green living" has greatly affected the building industry. Green carpentry attempts to reduce the amount of energy needed to complete a job, while also creating durable structures. New home designs can cut down on homeowners' energy needs by creating more efficient structures. New, environmentally friendly building materials have caused many carpenters to rethink the way they work. Green carpentry involves purchasing local materials and supplies. The long-distance shipment of carpentry materials and supplies is very harmful to the environment. The longer the distance, the greater the pollution created by

These carpenters are working on the roof of a green home, which was built to be environmentally friendly and energy-efficient.

forms of transportation. Contractors can buy supplies from local lumber yards and hardware stores. Better yet, they can reuse materials. Sometimes it is possible to take beautiful, old floorboards from a house that is being torn down and use them

in the construction of a new home across town. This can also be done with doorknobs, windowpanes, bricks, and so on.

Despite changes to the profession, carpentry has stayed largely the same for centuries. Carpenters build the world around us and make it a better place to live. Choosing to pursue a career in carpentry is a wise decision for someone who has the desire to succeed in the world today.

glossary

accredited Officially recognized by a governing body to perform a specified job. For instance, carpenters are accredited by the UBC.

associate's degree A two-year degree from a college.

blueprint A photographic print of a technical drawing.

commercial Relating to the world of business.

contractor A company or individual with a formal contract to do a specific job. Contractors supply labor, materials, and management staff during a job.

drywall A type of wall board made of sheets of plaster pressed together.

fabricate To construct something from different parts.

fiberglass A lightweight, durable building material made from compressed glass fibers.

Formica A strong plastic sheet used to protect surfaces.

freelance To work for several employers, rather than just one. Freelance workers often take on jobs with set time limits and, as a result, frequently look for new work.

industry Organized economic activity related to the production, manufacture, and construction of a specific type of product.

joiner A carpenter trained to make cuts in wood so that they fit together snugly without the use of nails or screws. Also used to describe carpenters who manufacture objects that need to have wood joints, such as door and window frames.

plumb bob A pointed weight suspended on the end of a string. Plumb bobs are used to create perfectly straight, vertical reference lines.

prefabricated Something that is manufactured in separate
  components that are intended to be assembled later.

residential Relating to private housing.

restoration To return something to the way it looked when
  it was first made.

scaffold A temporary framework of poles and planks used
  to support workers and their supplies.

strike When employees stop working as a group in order
  to protest a company's practices.

suspended ceiling A secondary ceiling hung below the main
  structural ceiling, which usually hides piping, wiring, and
  ductwork. Also called a dropped or false ceiling.

timber frame A kind of building constructed by fitting
  wooden beams together without nails and screws.

two-by-four A common size of lumber used for building
  projects. Two-by-fours are actually 1.5 inches (3.8
  centimeters) by 3.5 inches (8.9 cm) in dimension.

vocation A job or profession.

for more information

Associated Builders and Contractors (ABC)
4250 N. Fairfax Drive, 9th Floor
Arlington, VA 22203-1607
(703) 812-2000
Web site: http://www.abc.org
The ABC acts as the liaison between the construction indus-
    try and local, state, and federal governments, as well as the
    news media.

Associated General Contractors of America (AGC)
2300 Wilson Boulevard, Suite 400
Arlington, VA 22201
(703) 548-3118
Web site: http://www.agc.org
The AGC's mission is to help contractors and builders
    improve their businesses through education, increased
    job safety, and stronger government relations.

Canadian Construction Association (CCA)
75 Albert Street, Suite 400
Ottawa, ON K1P 5E7
Canada
(613) 236-9455
Web site: http://www.cca-acc.com
The CCA strives to improve industry practices and standards
    and to inform people about the construction industry.

Canadian Home Builders' Association (CHBA)
150 Laurier Avenue West, Suite 500

Ottawa, ON K1P 5J4
Canada
(613) 230-3060
Web site: http://www.chba.ca
The CHBA gives businesses in the home-building industry a
   voice in Canadian government. The association is con-
   cerned with numerous issues, including environmental
   protection, tax reform, and industry growth.

Employment and Training Administration (ETA)
U.S. Department of Labor
Frances Perkins Building
200 Constitution Avenue NW
Washington, DC 20210
(877) US-2JOBS [872-5627]
Web site: http://www.doleta.gov
Part of the U.S Department of Labor, the ETA is a federal
   organization that offers a wide range of training and
   apprenticeship services and resources.

Home Builders Institute (HBI)
1201 15th Street NW, Sixth Floor
Washington, DC 20005
(800) 795-7955
Web site: http://www.hbi.org
The HBI works to train men and women for careers in the
   construction industry.

Job Corps
200 Constitution Avenue NW, Suite N4463
Washington, DC 20210
(202) 693-3000
Web site: http://www.jobcorps.gov

The Job Corps is a program that helps train young people for careers in the workforce.

National Association of Women in Construction (NAWIC)
327 S. Adams Street
Fort Worth, TX 76104
(800) 552-3506
Web site: http://www.nawic.org
The NAWIC was created to represent women in the construction industry and provide them with a valuable support network.

United Brotherhood of Carpenters and Joiners
    of America (UBC)
International Headquarters
101 Constitution Ave NW
Washington, DC 20001
Web site: http://carpenters.org
The UBC is North America's largest construction trade union. The UBC offers extensive training resources and employment opportunities.

WEB SITES

Due to the changing nature of Internet links, Rosen Publishing has developed an online list of Web sites related to the subject of this book. This site is updated regularly. Please use this link to access the list:

http://www.rosenlinks.com/ecar/carp

for further reading

Bird, Lonnie. *Taunton's Complete Illustrated Guide to Using Woodworking Tools*. Newtown, CT: Taunton Press, 2004.

Burch, Monte. *Tool School: The Missing Manual for Your Tools*. Cincinnati, OH: Popular Woodworking Books, 2007.

Carpenter, Tom. *The Complete Book of Woodworking*. Urbandale, IA: Landauer Corporation, 2009.

Haun, Larry. *How to Build a House*. Newtown CT: Taunton Press, 2008.

Kelsey, John. *Woodworking*. East Petersburg, PA: Fox Chapel Publishing, 2008.

Korn, Peter. *Woodworking Basics: Mastering the Essentials of Craftsmanship*. Newtown, CT: Taunton Press, 2003.

Marshall, Chris. *The Complete Guide to Carpentry for Homeowners: Basic Carpentry Skills & Everyday Home Repairs*. Chanhassen, MN: Creative Publishing International, 2007.

McKee, Jack. *Woodshop for Kids*. Bellingham, WA: Hands-On Books, 2005.

Noble, David F. *Gallery of Best Résumés*. St. Paul, MN: JIST Works, 2007.

Noll, Terrie. *The Joint Book: The Complete Guide to Wood Joinery*. Secaucus, NJ: Chartwell Books, 2007.

Popular Woodworking. *Birdhouses You Can Build in a Day*. Cincinnati, OH: Popular Woodworking Books, 2004.

Robertson, Craig, and Barbara Robertson. *The Kids' Building Workshop: 15 Woodworking Projects for Kids and Parents to Build Together*. North Adams, MA: Storey Publishing, 2004.

Slomka, Beverly. *Teens and the Job Game: Prepare Today—Win It Tomorrow*. Bloomington, IN: iUniverse, Inc., 2007.

Stiles, David, and Jeanie Stiles. *Treehouses & Playhouses You Can Build*. Layton, UT: Gibbs Smith, 2006.

Strong, Jeff. *Woodworking for Dummies*. Hoboken, NJ: Wiley Publishing, 2004.

Svitil, Torene, and Amy Dunkleberger. *So You Want to Work in Set Design, Costuming, or Make-up?* Berkeley Heights, NJ: Enslow Publishers, 2008.

Thalon, Rob. *Graphic Guide to Frame Construction*. Newtown, CT: Taunton Press, 2009.

Vogt, Floyd. *Carpentry*. Clifton Park, NY: Delmar Learning, 2007.

bibliography

Associated General Contractors of America. "Construction Career Academy." Pamphlet. Arlington, VA: 2007.

Bureau of Labor Statistics. *Occupational Outlook Handbook, 2008–09 Edition*. Washington, DC: U.S. Department of Labor. Retrieved August 10, 2009 (http://www.bls.gov/oco).

Carpenters International Training Fund. "Superintendent Career Training Program." United Brotherhood of Carpenters. Retrieved August 10, 2009 (http://www. ubcsuperintendents.org/about.shtml).

Farr, Michael, and Laurence Shatkin. *200 Best Jobs Through Apprenticeships*. Indianapolis, IN: JIST Publishing, 2009.

Huth, Mark W. *Basic Principles for Construction*. Clifton Park, NY: Thomson Delmar Learning, 2008.

Miller, Mark R., Rex Miller, and Glenn E. Baker. *Construction and Carpentry*. New York, NY: McGraw-Hill, 2004.

Moskal, Greg. Telephone interview. July 20, 2009.

Porterfield, Deborah. *Top Careers in Two Years: Construction and Trades*. New York, NY: Infobase Publishing, 2007.

Sheldon, Roger. *Opportunities in Carpentry Careers*. New York, NY: McGraw-Hill, 2007.

United Brotherhood of Carpenters. "Sisters in the Brotherhood." Carpenters.org. Retrieved August 13, 2009 (http://www.carpenters.org/WhoWeAre/ SistersInTheBrotherhood/SistersInTheBrotherhood.aspx).

United Brotherhood of Carpenters. "Who We Are." Carpenters.org. Retrieved August 10, 2009 (http://www.carpenters.org/WhoWeAre).

U.S. Department of Labor. "Job Corps." Pamphlet. Washington, DC: 2009.

U.S. Millitary. "Military Mason and Carpentry Specialist." UsMilitary.com. Retrieved August 4, 2009 (http://www.usmilitary.com/4063/military-mason-and-carpenter-specialist).

Wasson, Julia. "Green Carpenter 'Turns Liabilities into Assets.'" *Blue Planet Green Living*, December 11, 2008. Retrieved September 8, 2009 (http://www.organicgreenandnatural.com/2008/12/11/green-carpenter-turns-liabilities-into-assets).

index

A

accidents in the workplace, 13, 14

apprenticeships, 21, 23, 29–32, 34–35, 37, 38, 39, 58

B

blueprints, 13, 17, 49, 51

building materials, 6, 10, 49, 52, 53, 54, 55, 59, 65

business, starting a, 61–63

C

cabinetmakers, 6, 7, 31, 51–53, 55, 59, 62, 63

career goals, 39–41

career schools, 17–19

Carpenters International Training Fund's Superintendent Career Training Program, 58, 60

carpentry
    career advancement in, 27, 58, 60–61
    career stability of, 5, 7, 20, 48, 63–67
    education in, 15–33, 43
    establishing a career in, 23, 39–48
    history of, 7–10
    safety and, 14
    skills needed in, 6–7, 8, 10–14, 34–35
    women in, 46

certification, 19, 27, 29, 33, 38

college education, 21–23, 25–26

commercial carpentry degree, 21

communication skills, 13

contractors, 21, 43, 53, 61–62, 67

correspondence courses, 27–28

cover letters, 45

E

Ellings, Margaret, 46

entertainment industry, 57, 58

F

finishers, 10, 51, 59

floor coverers, 53, 59

follow-up letters, 46

foremen, responsibilities of, 58

G

general equivalency diploma (GED), 25

ABOUT THE AUTHOR

Greg Roza has been creating educational materials for schools and libraries for ten years. He has a master's degree from SUNY Fredonia. Roza lives in Hamburg, New York, with his wife, Abigail, and their three children—Autumn, Lincoln, and Daisy. He has spent much of the last eight years fixing the home he bought and learning many valuable carpentry skills along the way.

PHOTO CREDITS

Cover, p.1 © www.istockphoto.com/laughingmango; cover (inset) © www.istockphoto.com/flyfloor; p. 4 © www.istockphoto.com/jimkruger; p. 7. Erich Lessing/Art Resource, NY; pp. 9, 12–13, 14 Shutterstock.com; pp. 11, 30 © www.istockphoto.com/Mel Stoutsenberger; pp. 16, 47, 50 © Michael J. Doolittle/The Image Works; pp. 18–19 © Douglas R. Clifford/St. Petersburg Times/Zuma Press; pp. 22–23, 54 © AP Images; pp. 24–25 © Steven Rubin/The Image Works; pp. 26, 56–57 © Jim West/Zuma Press; pp. 32–33 © David R. Frazier/The Image Works; p. 35 © Bryan Smith/Zuma Press; p. 36 Hulton Archive/Getty Images; pp. 40–41 Justin Sullivan/Getty Images; p. 42 Robin Bartholick/UpperCut Images/Getty Images; p. 44 Image Source/Getty Images; pp. 52–53 © www.istockphoto.com/George Peters; pp. 60–61 altrendo images/Stockbyte/Getty Images; pp. 64–65 Hill Street Studios/Blend Images/Getty Images; pp. 66–67 krtphotos/Newscom.com.

Designer: Matt Cauli; Photo Researcher: Amy Feinberg

WATERFORD TOWNSHIP
PUBLIC LIBRARY

DATE DUE

GAYLORD

PRINTED IN U.S.A.